The Aleister Crowley Encyclopedia

Harold Everett

© Copyright 2022 Harold Everett
All Rights Reserved

Contents

Introduction

Aleister Crowley was an iconoclast and fascinating figure who shocked society with his debauched and occult behaviour. Crowley is famous for his spiritual, magic and occult studies. He was called a dangerous Satanist but there are many layers and nuances to his mystical beliefs and his religious system called Thelema.

Crowley was a writer, poet, chess master, painter, spy, journalist, world traveller and mountain climber. He was a big recreational drug user and experimenter, and had a rather liberal attitude to sexual matters. His ideas and personality have inspired many artists, people and movements in modern times - such as the New Age movement, rock musicians and Wicca.

Find out more about Aleister Crowley, his colourful life and ideas with this book - The Aleister Crowley Encyclopedia.

A

A∴A∴

The A∴A∴ was an order founded by Crowley in 1907. The initials are the Latin for silver star.

It was founded with George Cecil Jones and intended to be a successor to the Hermetic Order of the Golden Dawn. The headquarters and temple were at 124 Victoria Street, London.

There were three orders in the society:

The Silver Star - the highest and the governing body

The Rosy Cross - the second order

The Golden Dawn - the first order

The initiations in the organisation are syncretic with aspects of Vedantic yoga, ceremonial magic and Thervada Buddhism. The groups mystical and magical methods of spiritual growth were under the Qabalistic tree of life structure.

Members work alone - this was to avoid disputes and political problems. Its teachings are based on individual student teacher relationships and there are no social organizations or fraternities in the order. Its central aim is "simply to lead each aspirant toward their own individual attainment, for the betterment of all humanity. The main book of the society is The Book of the Law, the holy book of Thelema.

Crowley published secret rituals from The Golden Dawn in the A∴A∴ journal The Equinox which upset Golden Dawn members. Crowley was sued in 1910 by one of the group's founders Samuel Liddell MacGregor Mathers for revealing Golden Dawn secrets; but Crowley won the court case. This attracted publicity to Crowley and the A∴A∴ and attracted some famous people to the group.

Crowley developed a magical performance performed by A∴A∴ members named Rites of Artemis at A∴A∴ HQ. After positive reviews the performance was tweaked and performed as Rites of Eleusis at Caxton Hall in London.

Later the O.T.O. declared the A∴A∴ to be an ally, and Crowley joined the O.T.O. in 1912.

After Crowley's death in 1947 there were several groups claiming linage from the A∴A∴.

Abbey of Thelema

In 1920 Crowley moved to Sicily to found a headquarters for his personal occult religion Thelema; it was based at the Abbey of Thelema in Cefalu, Sicily. The building for the abbey was an old villa called the Santa Barbara.

Crowley lived there in commune like conditions writing, painting and performing magical rituals often involving drugs and sexual acts. It was intended to be a school for Crowley's Thelemic teachings and magic with residents trying to find their own True Will.

In 1923 the Abbey was closed after Crowley was expelled from Italy by the Fascist government of Benito Mussolini because of his debauched magical activities activities at the Abbey. His activities caused a newspaper to call Crowley 'the wickedest man in the world.'.

English bohemian Betty May lived at the commune with her husband Raoul Loveday. She hated the commune and Crowley as Loveday had died at the Abbey during a ritual - probably from drinking contaminated spring water. She subsequently sold her story to John Ball making up stories about life at the commune. Crowley could not afford to sue, so the stories were repeated worldwide causing the Italian government to expel him.

Abrahadabra

Abrahadabra is a word created by Crowley. It first appeared in his 1904 book The Book of the Law. Crowley said the word meant

"the Word of the Aeon, which signifieth The Great

Work accomplished."

The Book of the Law, Crowley thought, created a new age - an Aeon - for man ruled by the Egyptian God Ra-Hoor-Khuit.

The word is similar to another magic related phrase: Abracadabra. Crowley replaced the c with an h as H refereed to the Egyptian God Horus in a Golden Dawn Neophyte ritual.

Also in the qabalistic method of gematria where letters are given numbered values, Abrahadabra gives a selection of results pertinent to Crowley's beliefs and studies. For example, ABRAHADABRA = 418, 418 = ΑΙΓΑΣΣ, a Greek spelling of Aiwass; Aiwass gave Crowley details of the Book of the Law.

Aeon

Aeon is an aspect of the Thelemic religion. Thelema believes that humanity is divided into Aeons. Each Aeon has its own religious expression and magical forms.

The First Aeon was the Aeon of Isis. This happened during prehistory starting in 2900 BC. Man worshiped a Great Goddess - which was the Egyptian deity Isis. There was a matriarchal society.

Crowley stated on the Aeon of Isis:

"simple, quiet, easy, and pleasant; the material ignores the spiritual."

Next was the Aeon of Osiris which ran from the medieval and classical periods from 500 BC. During this period the Egyptian God Osiris was worshiped - a male God. The Aeon was thus dominated by patriarchal vales. Crowley said of this Aeon:

"The second [Aeon] is of suffering and death: the spiritual strives to ignore the material. Christianity and all cognate religions worship death, glorify suffering, deify corpses".

The third and current Aeon is the Aeon of Horus. Which started in 1904. This coincided with the publication of Crowley's key work The Book of the Law. Horus the child God controlled the Aeon. Humanity achieves self realisation and self actualisation during this period. Individuality and working towards one's true will are important parts of this Aeon. In this period there is a large interest in spiritual matters. Some have suggested this has similar characteristics as the New Age or Age of Aquarius. Crowley says on this Aeon:

"The Aeon of Horus is here: and its first flower may well be this: that, freed of the obsession of the doom of the Ego in Death, and of the limitation of the Mind by Reason, the best men

again set out with eager eyes upon the Path of
the Wise, the mountain track of the goat, and
then the untrodden Ridge, that leads to the ice-
gleaming pinnacles of Mastery."

Aiwass

Aiwass is the name of a voice Crowley heard in
April 1904 in Cairo, Egypt.

His wife Rose Edith Kelly channelled the voice
which dictated text which was written down in The
Book of Law.

Crowley described the voice as being free from
any accent and of a musical and expressive
nature. Aiwiss was described as a tall man in his
30s and dressed in Assyrian clothing. He was
described as having more knowledge than any
human could possibly have.

Crowley called Aiwiss at times his own personal
holy Guardian Angel. Some have suggested that
Aiwiss is the unconscious manifestation of
Crowley's personality rather than a separate
entity.

Alexander VI

Pope Alexander VI was born Rodrigo de Borgia
and lived between 1 January 1431 – 18 August

1503. He was Pope between 11 August 1492 until his death in 1503. He was a controversial Pope, being known as a libertine. He had several children by different women and was said to organise orgies.

In 1501 Alexander VI organised an orgy known as the Banquet of Chestnuts. Alexander, his son and various acquaintances enjoyed the company of 50 prostitutes.

Alexander's master of ceremonies Johann Burchard wrote in his diary:

"There is no longer any crime or shameful act that does not take place in public in Rome and in the home of the Pontiff. Who could fail to be horrified by the...terrible, monstrous acts of lechery that are committed openly in his home, with no respect for God or man? Rapes and acts of incest are countless...[and] great throngs of courtesans frequent St. Peter's Palace, pimps, brothels, and whorehouses are to be found everywhere!"

He has been called the "most corrupt Pope in history".

Naturally all this appealed to Crowley. In 1918 he went on a magical retreat on Esopus Island on the Hudson River in New York State. It was an area of wilderness. Crowley claimed to have experienced past life memories of Pope Alexander VI here.

Amalantrah Working

Crowley embarked on a series of magical experiments in New York in 1917. They were termed the Amalantrah Working.

Crowley was trying to create a channel so extra terrestrial entities could contacted and conversed with. Crowley made contact with an alien called Lam. He sketched a picture of Lam. he alien looked similar to the Grey alien which looked surprisingly similar to the alien described in accounts of modern alien abductions and visitations. Some have suggested Crowley opened up a portal to enable Greys to visit Earth – and they have been visiting ever since.

Crowley put a portrait of Lam in his book Voice of the Silence. Why he did this is unknown - maybe Lam, was the chief of the A.A. or had a special connection with Crowley.

B

Babalon

Babalon or Scarlet Woman, Great Mother and Mother of Abominations is a goddess in Thelema. The name Babalon was revealed in the book The Vision and the Voice.

Babalon represents a liberated woman and the female sexual impulse. An avatar of Babalon is a living woman who has the title of Scarlet Woman. The Scarlet Woman must help create the energies for the Aeon of Horus (the current Aeon which began in 1904). The Scarlet Woman can be changed. Crowley wrote the Scarlet Woman is "replaceable as the need arises".

The male consort of Babylon is Chaos - the Father of Life in the Gnostic Mass.

The Babalon was inspired by the Whore of Babylon from the Book of Revelation - a book which influenced Crowley's Thelemic writings.

Those people Crowley considered to be his scarlet women were:

Rose Edith Crowley (Crowley's wife between 1903-09); Mary d'Este Sturges; Jeanne Robert Foster; Roddie Minor; Marie Rohling; Bertha Almira Prykrl and Leah Hirsig.

It has been suggested that Crowley chose emotional or women with mental health problems as they were more suited to magical pursuits.

Charles Henry Allan Bennett

Charles Henry Allan Bennett (8 December 1872 – 9 March 1923) was a Buddhist and a member of the Hermetic Order of the Golden Dawn.

Born in London, he had a Catholic upbringing but searched for other spiritual beliefs. Inspired by Sir Edwin Arnold's' book (1879) The Light of Asia, he became a Buddhist.

Crowley and Bennett first met in 1899 at an initiation ceremony for the Golden Dawn. Bennett agreed to teach Crowley about the occult. Crowley said:

"we were working together day and night, and a devil of a time we had!".

Crowley said that Bennett was a great inspiration to him. Bennett needed to go to Ceylon (Sri Lanka) as his doctor suggested the warmer climate was better for his various health problems. Crowley arranged the travel expenses - via an ex mistress as he did not want to offend Bennett by giving him charity.

In 1901 Crowley visited Bennett in Kandy in Sri Lanka and was impressed by his yoga skills - particularly the Lotus position.

In 1907 the two fell out after Crowley rejected Buddhism in favour of his own Thelemic religion; but Crowley still respected Bennett and his ideas.

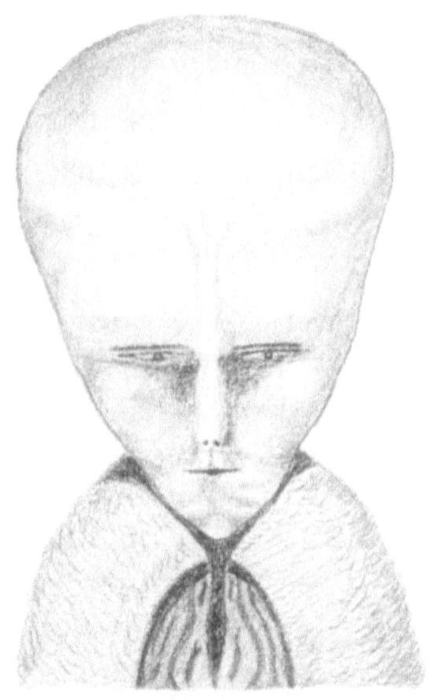

Lam

Bisexual

Aleister Crowley was a bisexual, although he "had a preference for women".

His relationships with men were much fewer than with women and mostly in his younger days.

Crowley's bisexuality was a part of his belief that there must be complete sexual freedom for men and women. Also Crowley thought that spiritual enlightenment came from not following sexual norms. Same sex acts played a big part in his magical rituals and his exploration of his spirituality and magic.

James Bond

It is said that Ian Fleming writer Ian Fleming based the character Le Chiffre on Crowley. Le Chiffre is a villain in the Casino Royale novel. He has a penchant for sadomasochism.

Fleming and Crowley were associates during World War 2 as Fleming worked for British intelligence and they considered using Crowley for some tasks. Rudolf Hess, Hitler's Deputy, flew from Germany to Scotland in 1941 in order to make peace. Hess was interested in occult matters such as astrology and magic. Therefore it was thought that Crowley would be a good person to interrogate Hess. It is debated whether Crowley and Hess actually met.

Perhaps Fleming was also inspired by Crowley for master criminal Blofeld. Blofeld was an exotic character often creating new outlandish personas for himself as was Crowley. Fleming's Live and Let Die also has occult themes – particularly as regards to voodoo.

The Book of Lies

The Book of Lies is a book by Crowley published in 1912. When it was first published Crowley used the pen name Pater Perdurabo. Crowley's muse at the time Leila Waddell helped with the book: she is called Laylah in the book.

The book consists of 91 one page chapters. Crowley said of the book:

"This book deals with many matters on all planes of the very highest importance. It is an official publication for Babes of the Abyss, but is recommended even to beginners as highly suggestive."

The chapter include poems, rituals, cryptograms and illusions. In 1921 Crowley wrote a commentary to help with a Qabalistic interpretation of each chapter.

The book includes Mass of the Phoenix ritual, which many famous magic practitioners have performed.

Book 77

Book 77 is a book by Crowley published in 1941. It is also known as Book 77. The book is 1 page in length and consists of five concise paragraphs.

The paragraphs are: moral, bodily, mental, sexual, and the safeguard tyrannicide.

The book was written for Louis Wilkinson to simply explain the O.T.O. plan.

Book of Thoth

Crowley published the Book of Thoth in 1944. In it he discussed tarot cards - in particular the philosophy and use of Crowley's Thoth Tarot Tarot cards deck which he designed with Lady Frieda Harris.

The original edition was limited to 200 signed and numbered copies. It was bound on Moroccan leather and Crowley made £1500 at 1044 prices of the printing.

The book is divided into four major parts:

Part One: The Theory of the Tarot.
Part Two: The Atu (Keys or Trumps).
Part Three: The Court Cards.
Part Four: The Small Cards.

Also included:

Appendix A: Tarot in the Art of Divination;

Appendix B Ober Dictum, Key Scale of the Tree of Life plus with the conic sections of mathematics and a diagram attributing the trigrams of the I Ching to the ten Sephirot.

C

Cambridge University

Crowley studied at Cambridge University between 1985-1898. He studied at Trinity College.

Crowley initially studied for the Moral Science Tripos before switching to study English literature. He spent a great deal of time reading classical literature. Crowley said:

"Nothing else seemed to me worth while but a thorough reading of the great minds of the past. I bought all the classical authors. Whenever I found a reference of one to another I hastened to order his works. I spent the whole of my time in reading. It was very rare that I got to bed before daylight."

It was at Cambridge that he developed his interest in the occult and mysticism. Crowley said he studied the abnormal and the "freak".

He intended to go into the diplomatic service, specialising in Russian affairs. But in 1897 after an illness decided to devote his life to magic.

As for his results, he passed the second part of the general Examination in the Michaelmas Term 1896, the first part in Easter Term 1897 and took the special Examination in Chemistry in the

Michaelmas term, 1897, obtaining a second class. He did not graduate.

In The Confessions of Aleister Crowley he wrote:

'Like Byron, Shelley, Swinburne and Tennyson, I left the university without taking a degree. It has been better so; I have accepted no honour from her; she has had much from me.'

Chess

Crowley was very interested in chess. At Cambridge he was President of the Chess Club and would play for several hours a day. He even considered a career as a chess player.

He was taught chess as a young boy by a tailor who was also a member of the Plymouth Brethren - the Christian religious group Crowley's parents belonged to. Crowley was apparently a quick learner.

Crowley stated that on returning from a trip to St Petersburg, Russia in 1897 he attended the Berlin Chess Congress. Crowley was not impressed with the chess players. He later wrote:

"I saw the masters — one, shabby, snuffy and blear-eyed; another, in badly fitting would-be respectable shoddy; a third, a mere parody of humanity, and so on for the rest. These were the people to whose ranks I was seeking admission. "There, but for the grace of God, goes Aleister Crowley,"

I exclaimed to myself with disgust, and there and then I registered a vow never to play another serious game of chess. I perceived with praeternatural lucidity that I had not alighted on this planet with the object of playing chess."

Crowley did not become a professional player, but enjoyed the game on a more casual basis throughout his life.

Children

Crowley had five children.

Lilith Crowley was born in 1905. She died in 1906 of typhoid in Rangoon. Lilith's full name was Nuit Ma Ahathoor Hecate Sappho Jezebel Lilith Crowley.

Lola Zaza was born in 1907. Lola was not on good terms with Crowley. She died in 1990 in Reading, England aged 84.

Crowley had a daughter named Anna Leah Poupée in 1920. She died aged only 9 months.

Louise Shumway was born in 1920 in Sicily. Crowley had called her Astarte Lulu Panthea. Her mother was Ninette Shumway - also known as Isabella Fraux. Louise died in 2014 in Oakland California. Louise led a normal life as a school teacher and was a Presbyterian.

Randall Gair was born in 1937. He died in 2002 aged 65 in a car accident. When Randall was born Crowley was 61 and Randall's mother Patricia Doherty was 22. Randall was nicknamed Aleister Ataturk. He suffered from schizophrenia and at one point wanted to take power in Britain as he thought he was Adjudicator of the Supreme Council of Great Britain which he believed was the legitimate British government.

Christmas

Did Aleister Crowley celebrate Christmas? As a child he was not allowed to celebrate Christmas as his family belonged to a Christian fundamentalist sect who believed Christmas to be pagan. Although Crowley criticised Christianity in his writings, there are many recorded incidents of him enjoying Christmas. Many can be found in his diaries.

For Christmas 1919 he spent the period with his Aunt Annie in Addiscombe, England. He enjoyed a traditional Christmas dinner. In The Magical Record of the Beast 666 he states that he enjoyed a traditional Christmas for 1914:

"A real Merrie Xmas, with roast beef and plum

pudding and old port and brandy."

For Christmas 1945 at Netherwood retirement house in England Crowley stated write in his diary that he judged a fancy dress competition.

Of course there is anecdotal evidence of Crowley playing up to his occult image by making fun of Christmas. One year he sent a Christmas card with "Happy Nirvana" on it. He is also to have said "Christians to the lions!" to carol singers.

Clouds without Water

Clouds without Water is a book of poetry written by Crowley and published in 1909.

It was published by Crowley's pseudonym Rev. C. Verey. It was claimed in the introduction to the book that the poems were from an anonymous manuscript that had recently been discovered.

In the notes Crowley writes as Verey, criticising the poems in a humorous manner.

The Confessions of Aleister Crowley

The Confessions of Aleister Crowley is a book written by Crowley. It is an autobiography which details his life until 1925. The full title is The Confessions of Aleister Crowley: An

Autohagiography; hagiographies are normally written about saints.

The book's sections are entitled:

Towards the Golden Dawn
The Mystical Adventure
The Advent of the Aeon of Horus
Magical Workings
The Magus
At the Abbey of Thelema

It was published as two volumes in 1929. He did not complete the autobiography. Several edited editions were released after Crowley's death.

D

Death

Aleister Crowley died on the 1st December 1947 at Netherwood House in Hastings, England.

He died of chronic bronchitis aggravated by pleurisy and myocardial degeneration. He was aged 72.

Crowley's funeral was held in Brighton, England at Brighton crematorium on the 5th December. Twelve people attended. Louis Wilkinson read passages from the Gnostic Mass, Hymn to Pan and The Book of the Law. Members of the press naturally made up lurid stories of occult ceremonies and a Black Mass at the funeral.

Crowley's ashes were buried by Karl Germer next to a tree in his garden in Hampton, New Jersey, USA. This later caused some controversy among Crowley's associates as in Crowley's Last Will and Testament he gave Germer instructions to preserve his ashes for posterity.

Diary

Crowley kept a diary of his magic and spiritual studies. he expected his students to keep one too.

Crowley noted down his diet, dreams, observations, spiritual exercises and other activities.

By writing down everything a practitioners of magic's abilities could be assessed. Also the diary could be used as the writer as a base for future studies and development.

The Diary of a Drug Fiend

The Diary of a Drug Fiend is a novel written by Crowley. It was first published in 1922. It was his first published novel.

The book is based on Crowley's own drug experiences and struggle with addiction. In the book World War 1 pilot Sir Peter Pendragon is a World War 1 veteran pilot who had inherited a large amount of money from his uncle.

He married the devotee of a leading occultist. They become addicted to cocaine and heroin, and travel around Europe.

With the help of magic rituals and the occult they battle their addictions and find their own Thelemic true will.

Dictum

Crowley's dictum was

'Do what thou wilt shall be the whole of the law.'.

The dictum was first mentioned in Crowley's 1909 book The Book of the Law.

The phrase refers to Thelema followers who should follow their own true path and determine their personal True Will.

Unicursal hexagram

Drugs

Crowley used drugs throughout his life: he was a recreational drug user.

He thought hashish in particular was an "aid to mysticism", and used this and other drugs to further his magical and spiritual experiences.

At his Rites of Artemis magic performances attendees were given punch with peyote.

In 1906 when he toured southern China he smoked opium constantly during the journey.

When Crowley lived in Sicily his heroin addiction became a huge problem, and according to reports his cocaine use eroded his nasal cavity. Crowley had numerous operations to repair his nose as a result.

Crowley tried to break his heroin addiction using his will. For example in 1922 he attempted a retreat in Paris to try and kick the habit. But heroin is a highly addictive drug and he remained a user.

In 1920 a Dangerous Drug Act was introduced in Britain making recreational drugs illegal. Crowley campaigned against the act. In Tunisia in 1923 he again tried to give up heroin. He managed to temper his heroin addiction. But, during World War 2 in 1940 Crowley was living in England and could not get his German made asthma medication. He used heroin instead.

During his retirement at Netherwood House in Hastings, England between 1945-47 Crowley took heroin for his asthma which he got from Heppel's chemist in London.

E

Ecclesia Gnostica Catholica

Ecclesia Gnostica Catholica is a Gnostic church organisation and the ecclesiastical arm of the O.T.O. and the Law of Thelema.

The main purpose of the group is the performance of the Gnostic Mass ritual which was written by Crowley in 1913 in Moscow, Russia. The mass is based on the Orthodox Christian and Roman Catholic masses.

Eucharist, confirmation, marriage, baptism and last rites are offered by the ritual. A goblet of wine and Cake of Light (a biscuit containing bodily fluids) is consumed. At the end of the ritual "There is no part of me that is not of the gods!" is said.

The ritual has always been a familiar part of O.T.O. gatherings.

Edward

Crowley was born as Edward Alexander Crowley. He changed his name to Aleister after a vision in Sweden.

Crowley said of his name change:

"For many years I had loathed being called Alick, partly because of the unpleasant sound and sight of the word, partly because it was the name by which my mother called me. Edward did not seem to suit me and the diminutives Ted or Ned were even less appropriate. Alexander was too long and Sandy suggested tow hair and freckles."

I had read in some book or other that the most
favorable name for becoming famous was one
consisting of a dactyl followed by a spondee, as at
the end of a hexameter: like Jeremy Taylor.

Aleister Crowley fulfilled these conditions and
Aleister is the Gaelic form of Alexander. To adopt
it would satisfy my romantic ideals."

Egypt

In 1904 Crowley claimed to have an important
vision in Egypt which gave him an image of a
"new era of humanity".

This vision provided a series of statements given
to Crowley and his wife Rose by a strange
presence named Aiwass. The statements were
recorded in The Book of the Law; published in
1909, it became the key text in the Thelema
religion.

In Cairo Crowley saw the Stele of Ankh-ef-en-
Khonsu, an Egyptian wooden painted stele from
680 AD. The painting became an important part
of the Thelemic religion and was called the Stele
of Revealing by Crowley. Its catalogue number
was 666 - a key number in Crowley's thinking,
and the three chief deities of Thelema were in the
painting: Nuit (Egyptian Nut), Hadit (Egyptian
Behdety), and Ra-Hoor-Khuit (Egyptian Re-
Harakhty)

During his visit to Cairo he took on the pseudonym of Prince Chioa Khan and took to dressing in a silk jacket and grew a long beard.

Eight Lectures on Yoga

Eight Lectures on Yoga is a book written by Crowley that was published in 1939. As the title suggests the book is about the practice of yoga. Astrology, physics, secret knowledge and other esoteric subjects are linked to yogic philosophy.

It is divided into two chapters: Yoga for Yahoos and Yoga for Yellowbelles. There are eight parts - based on lectures given by Crowley.

The book was intended to demystify myths about Yoga and be a simple guide; as a result it is considered to be one of the most readable of Crowley's writings.

Equinox

The Equinox was a magazine that was the official journal of Crowley's A∴A∴, and of Crowley's thought.

It was founded in 1909. Content included articles in magick and occultism as well as fiction, plays, poetry, biographies and artwork.

Between 1909 and 1913 it was published twice a year. There were six issues before Crowley died in 1947. Seven more issues were published after his death; the last issue was in 1998.

F

Father

Crowley's father was Edward Crowley. Born in 1829, he died in 1887 of tongue cancer. Aleister was aged 11.

Edward Crowley was an evangelical Christian. He had been born a Quaker but had converted to the fundamentalist group Plymouth Brethren; Edward Crowley had joined a more extreme branch of the sect called the Exclusive Brethren. He was also a travelling preacher. Crowley's mother joined the sect upon marriage to Edward. Crowley stated that he admired his father calling him a "hero and friend".

Edward had worked as an engineer. His share of the Crowley family brewing business Crowley's Alton Ales had allowed him to retire early.

Crowley inherited a third of his father's wealth which allowed Crowley to devote himself to his mystical pursuits and travel for numerous years.

Food

Crowley was a fan of spicy curried dishes, and would often make them for other at parties. A famous dish associated by Crowley is a very hot curried rice he would make during mountain climbing expeditions.

Crowley mixed in wealthy circles so naturally enjoyed dining at fine restaurants. One such example is a Hungarian dinner Crowley enjoyed with occult thriller writer Dennis Wheatley at the Hungaria restaurant in Lower Regent Street in London. Crowley gave Wheatley a book with the inscription "In memory of out sublime Hungarian banquet".

A favourite snack of Crowley's later in life was sardines sprinkled with curry powder.

Fraternitas Saturni

Fraternitas Saturni is a German magical order. Founded in 1926 its Latin name is Brotherhood of Saturn. The order accepts the Law of Thelema.

The order was founded at the Weida Conference in August 1925. This conference in Hohenleuben, Thuringa was convened to appoint Crowley as chief magus of German occult groups, consolidate his position as Outer Head of the O.T.O. and as a world teacher. Crowley attended the conference and discussed Thelema. Some did not like his teachings - especially as regards to sex magic; these people did not join the new order.

Fraternitas Saturni's founding was in 1928 in Berlin. The order followed the Book of Law but did not want to answer to Crowley. Rather than concentrate on Qabalah and Tarot the group placed more emphasis on Luciferian teachings and astrology.

The group was banned by the Nazis in 1936. It was re-founded after the war and is still in existence.

Freemasonry

Crowley claimed to be "initiated" into Freemasonry in Mexico City in 1900. He was a part of the Supreme Council of the Ancient and Accepted (Scottish) Rite. Crowley was initiated into the 33 degree of the Ancient and Accepted Rite. He obtained the title of Grand Inspector General. The only record of this appointment is by Crowley himself in his book The Confessions of Aleister Crowley. It has been said that Mexican and Central American Freemasonry at this time was disorganised with numerous unofficial short lived Masonic bodies being formed.

In 1904 Crowley was initiated into a Freemason's Lodge in France. The lodge was Anglo-Saxon

Lodge no. 343, under the jurisdiction of the Grande Loge de France.

Later John Yarker invited Crowley into his lodge. Yarker had been expelled from Masonic Supreme Council for setting up a grand council of the Ancient and Primitive Rite. Yarker set up his own Ancient and Primitive Rite and invited Crowley into the, giving him the 33, 90 and 95 degrees - the Ancient and Accepted, Memphis and Mizraim. Yarker and Crowley did not meet in person, and after Yarker died Crowley had a meeting in his flat in London to appoint himself Grand Administrator General and Patriarch Grand Conservator of the rite. His status was highered to 33, 90 and 96 degrees.

A draft letter written by Crowley in 1913 shows he asked the United Grand Lodge of England to give him the right to attend Masonic lodge meetings. But they did not allow him to attend lodge meetings regarding all the lodges Crowley had been associated with as "irregular bodies".

J.F.C. Fuller

J.F.C. Fuller (1876-66) was a British general and military historian. He was an expert strategist o armoured warfare which influenced key personalities on all sides during World War 2.

During the 1930s he supported Oswald Mosely

and his British Union of Fascists. He wrote after World War 2 that the wrong side had won the war calling Hitler the "saviour of the west".

Fuller held an interest in mysticism and the occult. In 1907 he had an essay published praising Crowley's poetry. The essay won a competition; Fuller's was the only entry. Fuller joined the A∴A∴. writing and editing documents and providing paintings for A∴A∴ literature which were well regarded.

In 1911 Crowley and Fuller fell out after Fuller expressed fears that Crowley's bisexuality would ruin Fuller's career. In 1913 issues of The Equinox's warned A∴A∴ members not to get magical training from Fuller and stated that he was no longer a member. Fuller continued to be interested in the occult. He later called Crowley a "genius", and after Crowley's death said:

 "Crowley was a genuine avatar, but I don't think he knew it, but I do think he senses it in an emotional way."

Furniture

There was a rumour that Crowley had furniture made from human skin in his house in Hastings at the end of his life. Was it true?

It was probably a macabre urban myth made up

by the town's residents.

G

Karl Germer

Karl Germer (1885-1962) was a German occultist.
Born in Germany he moved to the USA in 1927.

In America he was the Grand Treasurer General of
the O.T.O. responsible for raising funds for the
order.

In 1935 Germer's US visa expired. He moved to
Germany then under Nazi rule. Some supporters
of Crowley thought Hitler would be amenable to
Crowley's ideas and writings. But upon the
outbreak of World War 2 in 1939 Crowley's books,
such as The Book of the Law, and books on
qabalah, gematria, astrology and esotercism were
banned.

Germer was arrested by the Nazis in 1935
because of his occult links. His America wife Cora
asked the American authorities to look into his
case. Germer was freed because of his World War
1 record and moved to Belgium. After World War
2 started Germany invaded Belgium and he was
again imprisoned in several internment and
concentration camps. During his spell in
concentration camps he would recite the Holy

Books of Thelema to himself.

He he was released in February 1923 and returned to the USA. He remained a devoted supporter of Crowley and raised a lot of money for him in his role as the Grand Treasurer General of the O.T.O. For his support and fundraising abilities Crowley named Germer as his successor as head of the O.T.O. Crowley died in 1947 and Germer duly took up leadership of the O.T.O. He worked on preserving Crowley literary works and getting unpublished works published. He continued to work for the O.T.O. In letters just before his death he stated that he wanted during his life to support Crowley's ideas and publish his works.

Germer died in 1962. In his will he left all Crowley materials to the O.T.O.

Kenneth Grant

Kenneth Grant (1924-2011) was an English ritual magician and associate of Crowley's.

As a youngster Grant was interested in Western esotericism, occultism and Eastern religions. He wrote numerous letters to Crowley and eventually met him for the first time at the Bell Inn pub in Buckinghamshire, England.

Grant became Crowley's unpaid secretary, being

paid in magical instruction. Grant became a high initiate of the O.T.O. and Crowley saw him as a future British leader of the group. Grant left his work as Crowley's secretary in 1945 as it was unpaid. Crowley and Grant had argued on many occasions, and Crowley had said of Grant "I may have treated him too severely".

Grant attended Crowley's funeral in 1947.

Grant continued his studies of magic and Eastern religions, involved in his own faction of the O.T.O.

In the 1970s he edited a number of Crowley books for re-publication helping to bring a new wave of interest in Crowley. He was a prolific writer on magic and was key and influential figure in western occult thinking and study.

Greatest Britons

In a BBC poll of of the greatest people from Britain entitles 100 Greatest Britons, Crowley was ranked seventy third (Winston Churchill topped the poll).

The poll was conducted by the BBC in 2002. Ratings were determined via a television poll.

Crowley's inclusion was thought to be controversial.

Great Work

The Great Work is a term used in Hermiticism and Crowley's Thelemic tradition. It's Latin Translation is Magnum Opus. When the Great Work is accomplished, self-trancesdence is completed in its entirely. It is the ending of the spiritual path, the gaining of enlightenment and "the rescue of the human soul from the unconscious forces which bind it.".

In Thelema the Great Work is the union of the self and the All with the accomplishment of True Will through a number of varied spiritual practices.

Crowley stated that the Great work is a "conscious process" of spiritual growth, and the whole spiritual process rather than one specific moment. The path to accomplish the mystical union of the True Self with the All given by Crowley is to attain mystical enlightenment by studying subjects such as Hermetic Qabalah and alchemy, meditation, tarot, yoga and other form of ceremonial magick.

The studies in the Great Work process must be integrated into one's daily life as an ongoing process.

An inspiration for Hermite societies Eliphans Levi described the Great Work thus:

"The Great Work is, before all things, the creation

of man by himself, that is to say, the full and entire conquest of his faculties and his future; it is especially the perfect emancipation of his will."

Leila Waddell

H

Hadit

Hadit is a Thelemic deity. Hadit is the mail speaker in chapter two of the Book of the Law. Hadit informs the reader that he is the axle of the wheel, the cube in the circle, the flame that burns in the heart of man: the worshipper's inner self. Hadit is the Elixer Vitae - the inner spirit of man, Holy Ghost, DNA from sperm.

Hadit represents each point experience making up the sum of all experience. Hadit represents the secret individuality in every man.

Hastings

Crowley spent his last days living in Hastings at Netherwood, a boarding house and Victorian retirement home. He lived in the town between 1945-47.

He is said to have cursed Hastings, stating that you can never leave the town, always being forced to come back. One method Crowley suggested to break the curse was to take a "stone with a hole" from the beach when leaving.

Crowley applied to a member of the Hastings Chess Club: but his membership was turned down three times.

Locals stated that Crowley haunted the Robert De Mortain pub, which is no longer open. There is a Crowley's bar in the city which is said to contain Crowley's ghost - a shaven headed looking spectre of Crowley.

Hermetic Order of the Golden Dawn

The Hermetic order of the Golden Dawn was a society which Crowley joined in 1898. The society, founded in 1887, was a magical order which studied the occult, metaphysics and paranormal. It is said to have been a big influence on the modern Pagan tradition Wicca.

The Golden Dawn had three orders.

The first order taught esoteric philosophy, tarot, geomancy and astrology.

The second order taught magic, astral travel, scrying and alchemy.

The third order consisted of highly skilled secret chiefs.

Members included W.B. Yeats, Arthur Machen and Algernon Blackwood. When Crowley was initiated into the order he was initiated as Frater Perdurabo ("I will endure"). After a few years as a leading member Crowley was expelled after arguments and disputes with other people in the society. Crowley even accused Yeats of using black magic directed at him during the quarrels.

Crowley formed his own society the A∴A∴ in 1907. The Hermetic order of the Golden Dawn became less popular and divided after Crowley's exit.

Leah Hirsig

Leah Hirsig (April 9, 1883 – February 22, 1975) was an American Swiss woman who had an association with Crowley. Swiss born, she moved to New York aged 2.

As a child Hirsig had an interest in the occult. In 1918 she visited Crowley who was living in Greenwich Village in Manhattan. They immediately connected.

Crowley painted several portraits of her; she asked Crowley to paint her as a "dead soul". In 1919 Crowley consecrated her as his Babalon - Scarlet Woman. Her name was Alostrael. Alosrael means the grail/womb of God.

In her diary Hirsig wrote:

 "I dedicate myself wholly to The Great Work [Thelemic thought]. I will work for wickedness, I will kill my heart, I will be shameless before all men, I will freely prostitute my body to all creatures".

Hirsig helped Crowley to found his Abbey of Thelema in Cefalu in Sicily in 1920. Crowley and Hirsig signed the lease for the Abbey building as Sir Alastor de Kerval and Contessa Lea Harcourt.

Hirsig took part in sex magic rituals with Crowley. Crowley thought she was a very important magical partner and assistant in his spiritual experiments. In 1921 she presided over his attaining of the grade of Ipsissimus.

Also in Sicily was Crowley and Hirsig's daughter Anne Leah (nicknamed Poupee). Unfortunately she died aged only 8 months.

In 1924 Crowley and Hirsig parted. she continued studying Thelema and served as Crowley's secretary for a period in 1925.

In 1926 Hirsig's sister Marian Dockerill (Anna Maria Hirsig) wrote articles criticising Crowley calling him a cult leader, one being titled "My Life in a Love Cult, A Warning to All Young Girls".

Hirsig is said to have rejected Crowley as a prophet, while still following Thelema. She returned to work as a schoolteacher, passing away in Switzerland in 1975.

Holy Days

Thelema has several holy days in which followers can celebrate their beliefs.

March 20. The Feast of the Supreme Ritual. This celebrates the Invocation of Horus. This ritual was performed by Crowley on this date in 1904 to inaugurate the New Aeon of Horus.

March 20/March 21. The Equinox of the Gods: The Thelemic New Year (although some celebrate the New Year on April 8).

April 8 - April 10. The Feast of the Three Days of the Writing of the Book of the Law. This commemorated the writing of The Book of the Law by Aleister Crowley. A typical celebration is to read a chapter at noon on each day.

June 20/June 21. The Summer solstice in the Northern Hemisphere and the Winter solstice in the Southern Hemisphere.

August 12. The Feast of the Prophet and His Bride. This commemorates the marriage of Aleister Crowley and his first wife Rose Edith Crowley. Rose assisted in the writing of The Book of the Law.

September 22/September 23. The Autumnal equinox in the Northern Hemisphere and the Vernal Equinox in the Southern Hemisphere.

December 21/December 22. The Winter solstice in the Northern Hemisphere and the Summer Solstice in the Southern Hemisphere.

The Feast for Life, celebrated at the birth of a Thelemite follower and on birthdays.

The Feast for Fire/The Feast for Water. These feast days are when a child reaches puberty and begins to be an adult. The Feast for Fire is celebrated for a male, and the Feast for Water for a female.

The Feast for Death, celebrated on the death of a Thelemite and on the anniversary of their death. Crowley's Death is celebrated on December 1.

Holy Guardian Angel

The Holy Guardian Angel is central to the philosophy and practices of Thelema. The concept of a guardian angel protecting and guiding a person is an old one present in many religions, for example Christianity where guardian angels are frequently depicted in popular culture. Crowley considered the Holy Guardian Angel to be representative if one's truest divine order. Crowley sated late is in life that the Holy Guardian Angel is an independent being which may have been human at one time.

Crowley said that it was an important task of a magical practitioner to connect with their guardian angel.

It should never be forgotten for a single moment that the central and essential work of the Magician is the attainment of the Knowledge and Conversation of the Holy Guardian Angel. Once he has achieved this he must of course be left entirely in the hands of that Angel, who can be invariably and inevitably relied upon to lead him to the further great step—crossing of the Abyss and the attainment of the grade of Master of the Temple..

Crowley wrote a ritual called Liber Samekh for attaining the Knowledge and Conversation of one's guardian angel.

The Holy Books of Thelema

The Holy Books of Thelema is an anthology of books. There are 15 works in the anthology.

The anthology was first published in 1909 under a Greek name Θελημα. In 1983 the books were republished as The Holy Books of Thelema.

I

Ipssissimus

Ipssissimus is the highest order in the Order of the Golden Dawn. An Ipssissimus state is "beyond the comprehension" of those in the lower degree classes. A person in the Ipssissimus state lives in balance with the universe and is free from limitations.

Although the achievement of this grade must be

kept secret, Crowley declared himself Ipssissimus beyond the Gods in 1921.

Israel Regardie

Israel Regardie (1907-1985) was an English magician, occultist and writer.

Regardie was born in a Jewish family in London's East end. In 1921 he moved to Washington D.C. with his family. He became interested in the occult and esoterica reading Helena Blavataky's works as well as books on yoga, Hinduism and Buddhism.

In 1926 he wrote to Crowley's via his publisher about yoga. Regardie was initiated into the Washington College of the Societas Rosicruciana in America. In 1928 Crowley asked Regardie to become his secretary in Paris. Crowley asked Regardie to learn about the occult for himself and visit prostitutes to overcome his sexual inhibitions. Regardie did so and caught gonorrhea.

In 1929 Regardie's sister was concerned that Crowley may be responsible when Regardie was in hospital and contacted the police. The police found Regardie did not have an identity card and he was expelled. Regardie moved to Belgium, then moved to Kent, England with Crowley. But Crowley could not afford to keep him as his secretary and they parted as friends.

In the 30s Regardie wrote several books on occultism, causing offence by giving away secrets of the secret occult societies. In 1937 he moved back to the US. Regardie was interested in St Francis of Assisi and started calling himself Francis. He sent Crowley a copy of his latest book. Crowley wrote back calling him Frank and making an anti-Semitic insult. Regardie was angry and wrote back called him Alice and a "contemptible". They fell out and Crowley send a document attacking Regardie to other occultists.

Between 1938-40 Aries Press published four volumes of material from the golden Dawn edited by Regardie. This book was to become a classic and many used it to set up their own Golden Dawn groups. Crowley called the book theft and other occultists were annoyed that secret material had been published.

Regardie served in World War 2, then after the war gained a doctorate in psychology. He became a chiropractor using psychology to treat patients. Regardies edited books about Crowley and in 1970 wrote his own biography of Crowley after being unimpressed by other biographies. In 1970 The Eye in the Triangle: An Interpretation of Aleister Crowley was published. It went up to 1914 and was a book which balanced the positive aspects of Crowley with his faults.

His books became popular in the 1960s, and his house was burgled several times by Crowley fans looking for secret Golden Dawn material. In 1984 he wrote the 1000 page The Complete Golden Dawn System of Magic. Regardie's writings, teachings and publishing of Golden Dawn material are said to have "provided much of the foundation for modern Western occultism".

J

George Cecil Jones

George Cecil Jones (10 January 1873 – 30 October 1960) was an associate of Crowley. It is said he helped a young Crowley develop his interest in magick. He was a chemist by profession.

In 1895 he became a member of the Hermetic Order of the Golden Dawn in 1895. He introduced Crowley to the organisation. He co-founded the A∴A∴ in 1906 with Crowley. Jones contributed to the book Qabalah, 777 and other Qabalistic writings. Jones was close to Crowley and in 1909 was a trustee in a trust fund for Crowley and his daughter Lola Zara.

In October and November 1910 the A∴A∴ staged the Rites of Eleusis at Caxton Hall in Westminster. This gained a lot of press coverage. One paper The Looking Glass had an article which discussed Crowley's and his associates rather salacious private life and implied that Jones was a homosexual by association; although the article did not directly call Jones a homosexual. Homosexuality of course was illegal at the time in Britain. Crowley and others mentioned in the article declined to sue. Jones decided to sue for libel. Crowley was not called as a witness which did not help Jones's cases. Jones lost the case after the prosecution argued that Jones was guilty by association with Crowley. The prosecution lawyer stated:

"If a man values his own reputation so cheaply that he does not mind associating with that kind of creature [Crowley], he must not complain if comment is made about it".

The jury and judge agreed and the article was termed fair comment. Jones and Crowley drifted apart after the case and did not speak to each other again.

K

Kanchenjunga

In 1905 Aleister Crowley took part in a mountaineering expedition to climb the summit if Kanchenjunga in the Himalayas. Crowley wanted to break the altitude record.

Jules Jacot-Gullarmod, a Swiss doctor and photographer had the idea for the expedition. Jacot-Gullarmod recruited Alexis Pache and Charles-Adolphe Reymond for the climb' Crowley got Italian Alcesti C. Rigo de Righi as transport officer. Crowley and Jacot-Gullarmod fell out during the climb de to Crowley's treatment of the porters. Alexis Pache died in an avalanche along with three porters. Crowley showed no concern or sympathy and said Pache should not have been descending.

Later Crowley claimed to have reached 25,000 feet/7,620 m and broken the altitude record - which was broken in 1922 with the British expedition to Mount Everest which reached 8,320 feet.

Jacot-Guillarmod later got money off Crowley blackmailing him by saying he would release some of Crowley's pornographic poetry.

Edward Kelley

Edward Kelley (1 August 1555 – 1597) was an English occultist and medium. He was a keen investigator of magic and alchemy, and his colourful private life and work gives a notoriety.

Crowley was inspired by Kelley, particularly in the early 1900's and saw himself as the incarnation of Kelley.

Rose Edith Kelly

Rose Edith Kelly (1874-1932) married Crowley in 1903. She was his first wife. They divorced in 1909. Initially it was a marriage of convenience - Crowley married her to save her from an arranged marriage. But they grew closer after marriage.

In 1904 they took a trip to Egypt which served as an extended honeymoon. Rose undertook the Bornless Ritual, entering a trance and saying "they are waiting for you" to Crowley. For three days in April 1904 Rose asked him to sit down for one hour each day at noon and dictate words from a strange presence known as Aiwass. These words made up The Book of Law.

Rose and Crowley had two daughters: Nuit Ma Ahathoor Hecate Sappho Jezebel Lilith (1904–06) and Lola Zaza (1907–90).

Konx Om Pax

Konx Om Pax is a book written by Crowley which was published in 1907. The phrase Konx Om Pax comes from the Egyptian phrase Khabs-am Pekht which means "light rushing out in a single ray. This phrase is used in the Hermetic Order of the Golden Dawn's Vernal and Autumnal Equinox ceremonies.

There is a distinctive cover image of Konx Om Pax

written in stretched text; it was designed by Crowley under the influence of hashish.

The book has an introduction with quotations from figures such as Jesus, Dante and Catullus. The Wake World is an allegory with a magician ascending through the Kabbalistic Tree of Life,.

Thien Tao, or, the Synagogue of Satan is a parody in which a Crowley character asks people to learn something contrary to their natural tendency - i.e. a prude learning sexual expression.

Ali Sloper, or, the Forty Liars: A Christmas Diversion is a play mocking Ali Baba ad the 40 Thieves and a dialogue based on a conversation with Crowley and a friend on Christmas Day.

Stone of the Philosophers Which Is Hidden in the Mountain of Abiegnus is a satirical dialogue between a number of men each contributing a poem as part of a philosophical debate.

L

The Law is for All

The Law is for All Is a book by Aleister Crowley. It is a collection of his commentary on The book of the Law. It was edited to remove more complex qabalistic explanations on gematria and The Tree of Life.

The aim of the book is to guide the reader on the discovery of his own true will. Crowley reviewed the text before his death in 1947.

The book was published in 1974 as Magical and Philosophical Commentaries on the Book of the Law and edited by John Symonds and Kenneth Grant. Israel Regardie published another edition in 1985. In 1996 a version based on the 1947 manuscript was released.

Law of Thelema

The Law of Thelema was Crowley's philosophy. It was, according to Crowley, dictated to him by an ancient Egyptian spirit.

It was a philosophy which called for the pursuit of an individual's will unconstrained by conventional ethics or laws. Thelema was a translation of a Greek word meaning will.

It has been said that Thelema influenced Wicca and other modern pagan beliefs. Some have even suggested that Thelema influenced Scientology.

The main beliefs of Thelema are that one should follow ones own path: "Do what thou shall be the whole of the law". A person's will is like a star in the universe occupying a time and position in space with an independent nature: "Every man and every woman is a star". A person must find their own purpose in life and the nature of Thelema is love: "Love is the law, love under will".

The first outline of Thelema was in The Book of the Law, first published in 1909.

Liber Aleph

Liber Aleph vel CXI: The Book of Wisdom or Folly is a book by Crowley. It is the title of The Equinox, volume III, number VI. It is a letter to his magical son Frater Achad - Charles Stansfeld Jones.

It is written in the style of an epistle; there are 208 epistles in the book on various aspects of Thelema.

Libri of Aleister Crowley

The Libri of Aleister Crowley is a collection of written works by Crowley. Most are written or adapted by Crowley. Some of the works are by other authors. The collection is for students of Crowley's order the A∴A∴ and the O.T.O. Each Liber is given a Roman number.

The works are put in one of five classes.

Class A is for books that can't be changed as they represent the utterance of an Adept and are beyond criticism.

Class B is for books and essays from ordinary scholarship.

Class C is for suggestive books.

Class D is for official instructions and rulebooks.

Class E is for broadsheets and public announcements.

Some publications are in more than one class, or even not assigned a class.

Little Essays Toward Truth

Little Essays Toward Truth is a book by Crowley written in 1938.

The book contains 16 philosophical essays on various topics. such as Thelema and Qabalah. Topics include Sorrow, Love, Chastity and Truth.

Loch Ness

In 1899 Crowley bought a house by the Scottish lake of Loch Ness called Boleskine House. It had been built in the 1760s as a hunting lodge. He bought Boleskine House for twice its value. Upon buying the house Crowley gained the title of Laird of Boleskine. What attracted Crowley to the house was the occult architecture of the building, as well as the isolation of the building.

Crowley said:

"I had picked out Boleskine for its loneliness. Lord Lovat and Mrs Fraser-Tytler, my nearest neighbours, were eight miles away, while Grant of Glenmoriston was on the other side of Loch Ness."

Crowley wanted to use the house to perform an 18 month magic ritual called Abra-Melin. This ritual needed odd architecture so Boleskine was a good place for the ceremony. Abra-Melin is a 13th century north African ritual. A Jewish magician called Abraham translated the ritual from a rite given to him by the mage Abra-Melin. The Abra-Melin ritual summoned a guardian angel and summoned and bind the four Dukes of Hell - Satan, Belial, Leviathan and Lucifer.

His attempt to perform the ritual at Boleskine was not entirely successful, but strange occurrences started to happen at the house. Crowley had to sell the house because of financial problems in 1918 - at the end of the First world War.

Jimmy Page from the music group Led Zepplin bough the house and owned it from 1970-1992 as he was a fan of Crowley.

Later it was turned in a hotel, but various fires have ruined it. It is a listed building and may be restored in future.

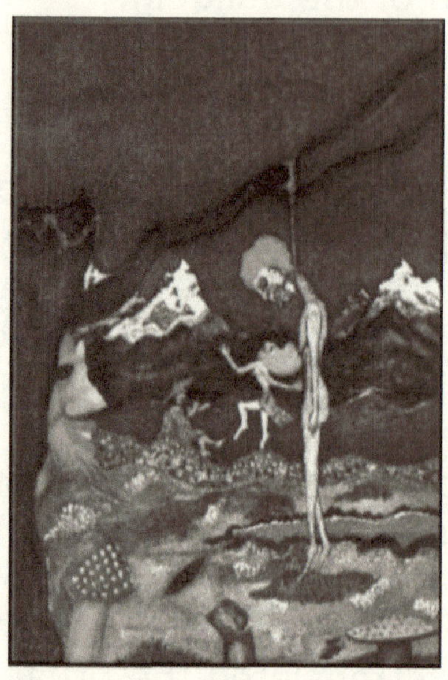

Crowley's painting May Morn

M

The Magician

W. Somerset Maugham had a Crowley type character in his 1908 novel The Magician. The novel published in 1908 is about a magician called Oliver Haddo who attempts to create life.

Maugham had met Crowley in Paris, and Haddo is considered a caricature of Crowley. In 1956 Maugham said the book was not one of his great works written in a "lush and turgid" style.

Crowley wrote a review of the book in Vanity Fair magazine in 1908 entitled How To Write a Novel (After W. S. Maugham). He criticised the book accusing Maugham of plagiarising such works as The Island of Dr Moreau by H.G. Wells in the novel.

Magick

Crowley added a k to the end of the word magic to create the word magick. One reason given for this is to differentiate real magic from stage magic.

Also magick is a six letter word; six sided shapes, hexagrams, are an important part of Crowley's beliefs.

Magick (Book 4)

Magick (Book 4) is a book by Crowley. He first published the book in 1912-13 in his magazine The Equinox (No VII).

The book is a treatise on Crowley's view on magick. The book consists of four parts:

Mysticism, Magick (Elementary Theory), Magick in Theory and Practice, and ΘΕΛΗΜΑ—the Law (The Equinox of The Gods). Also included are appendices with essays and rituals.

In 1911 Crowley undertook a ritual and was asked to write the book by an entity named Abildiz. He wrote the book at his house in Posillipo near Naples in Italy. His seer Soror Virakam (Mary Desti) assisted.

Magick Without Tears

Magick Without Tears is a book written by Crowley. It was written in 1943 and published in 1954 after Crowley had died. It was his last book.

The book contains 80 letters which are aimed at students of magick. Each letter has a different topic, such as yoga, death and the O.T.O..

Mandrake Press

Mandrake Press was a small publishing firm which Crowley owned. It was founded in 1929, Crowley bought it in 1930 and it was dissolved in 1930.

The company published the Crowley publications The Stratagem and other Stories, The Confessions of Aleister Crowley volumes I and II, and Moonchild.

Samuel Liddell MacGregor Mathers

Samuel Liddell MacGregor Mathers (11 January 1854 – 5 or 20 November 1918) was an occultist from Britain.

Mathers became leader of the Hermetic Order of the Golden Dawn in 1891. He was expelled in 1900. When leader of the Golden Dawn he introduced a rare rule for secret societies that women were allowed to be members on an equal basis. Crowley was initiated into the London branch of the order in 1898. Mathers agreed to initiate Crowley into the Second Order of the Golden Dawn, although other leading members of the Dawn did not agree with this and this led to disputes within the order.

Mathers and Crowley eventually fell out. They engaged in magical warfare. Crowley sent an army of demons to attack Mathers. In return Mather unleashed an astral vampire on Crowley.

Mathers thought he was losing control of the London branch of the Golden Dawn. He sent Crowley to take control of the London premises and equipment. But Crowley failed and he was expelled along with Mathers.

In 1909 Crowley attempted to publish the Golden Dawn secret rituals in his magazine The Equinox. Mathers sued in a case which gained lots of publicity; but Crowley won.

Mass of the Phoenix

Mass of the Phoenix is a single person magic ritual written by Crowley as part of Thelema. In the ritual the magician eats a Cake of Light containing blood and human semen.

Grady Louis McMurtry

Grady Louis McMurtry (1918-85) was an American occultist who was a student of Aleister Crowley.

He studied engineering and was introduced to Thelema by Jack Parsons. In 1941 he was initiated into the Minerval and I° of Ordo Templi Orientis (O.T.O.).

McMurty served during World War 2, taking part in D-Day. In preparation for D-Day he was stationed in England between 1943-44. It was here he met Crowley. Crowley made him IX° of O.T.O., and gave him the name of Hymenaeus Alpha. After Crowley's death in 1947 McMurty fell out with Crowley's successor as head of the O.T.O. Karl Germer. Germer refused to initiate new members which McMurthy opposed.

Germer died in 1962 and did not name a successor as O.T.O. head. Several people claimed to be head of O.T.O.

In 1969 O.T.O. member Phyllis Seckler wrote to

McMurty stating that there had been a burglary at the Crowley archives which were in the care of Germer's widow In California. In 1947 Crowley had sent McMurty a letter making him a Caliph (successor) of Crowley and appointed him Crowley's representative in the US. In 1969 he used this letter to claim leadership of the O.T.O. Based in California he revived the O.T.O. and it again had lodges and members all over the World.

McMurty died in 1985.

Mönch

In July 1896 Crowley made the first ever ascent of the Mönch mountain alone without a guide. The Mönch - the Monk - is mountain in in Bernese Alps in Switzerland. It is 4,110 metres/13480 feet. It is next to the Jungfrau and Elgar mountains.

Crowley wrote a poem titled 'A Descent of the Moench' on the climb.

Moonchild

Moonchild is a novel by Crowley written in 1917. The book is about a magical war between black and white magicians who are fighting over an unborn child. The hero of the book white magician Cyril Grey is based on Crowley.

Mother

Crowley's mother was Emily Bertha Bishop. She was born in 1848 and came from the west country of England - Devon and Somerset. She was a dogmatic Christian and said to be "humourless". She was a member of the strict Plymouth Brethren sect.

Naturally Crowley did not have a close relationship with his mother and called her "brainless bigot of the most narrow, logical and inhuman type".

Emily referred to her son as "The Beast 666, a title that Crowley revelled in.

Emily died in 1917.

Motto

Crowley's motto was Perdurabo. It means I shall endure to the end".

N

Netherwood

Crowley spent his final years at a boarding house

called Netherwood in the southern English coastal town of Hastings.

Netherwood was run by Vernon and Kathleen Symonds. The house had four acres of gardens with a tennis court. Beachy Head was nearby. The residents included painters, musicians and poets. Although Britain still had rationing of food at the time of Crowley's residence the cuisine at Netherwood was first class.

Crowley was having trouble finding somewhere to live in his later years due to his reputation. A friend, Louis Wilkinson, arranged for Crowley to live at Netherwood. Crowley moved in in September 1945. He was nearly 70 years old.

In 1970 the house closed and the building fell into a state of disrepair. Because of Crowley's connection to the house and because of the nature of the building, it gained a reputation as a haunted house. The building was turned into houses and the site had a pub called Robert De Mortain. The roof of the pub was torn off in 1987 in a great storm. Local witches claimed Crowley's spirit had something to do with it.

Victor Benjamin Neuburg

Victor Benjamin Neuburg (1883 – 1940) was an English writer and poet. He was interested in occultism and was an associate of Crowley.

He met Crowley in 1906. Neuberg was initiated into the A∴A∴ and took the magical name of Frater Omnia Vincam. He had a friendship and sexual relationship with Crowley taking part in sex magick rituals. The two fell out in 1914. It is said that Crowley would make anti-Semitic remarks about the Jewish Neuberg.

New Age

The New Age movement is made up of a variety of religious and spiritual beliefs that became popular in the west in the 1970s. New Age is a loose term to describe a zeitgeist of alternative ideas. It is a form of western esotericism taking inspiration from belief systems and practices such as the occult, channelling, eastern religions, alternative medicine, paganism, astrology and UFO inspired religions.

Crowley's interest in alternative beliefs and ideas and countering his contemporary culture meant that he was an inspirations for many of the ideas in the New Age.

Night of Pan

In the Thelema system night of Pan is a mystical state in the process of spiritual attainment that represents the stage of ego death. Pan is the Greek god of lust, nature and masculine generative power. He is a giver and taker of life.

The Night of Pan is a state where a person transcends all limitations and experiences one with the universe. The ego self is destructed.

The night is also called N.O.X. - N is the Tarot symbol of death and X is the sign of the Phallus.

Netherwood House

93

The number 93 has a big significance in Crowley's Thelema belief system. 93 refers to two key phrases: "do what thou wilt shall be the whole of the law" and "love is the law, love under will". Using the Greek isopsephy which gives a letter a numerical value "will"and "love" each come to 93.

"Thelema: Θελημα = 9 + 5 + 30 + 8 + 40 + 1 = 93
Agapé: Αγαπη = 1 + 3 + 1 + 80 + 8 = 93

The first phrase is abbreviated to "93" while the second is abbreviated to "93 93/93", with the division "93/93" symbolising love "under" will."

O

Obeah and Wanga

Obeah and Wanga are African native words that are used in The book of the Law.

Also the mantras and spells; the obeah and the wanga; the work of the wand and the work of the sword; these he shall learn and teach. (AL I:37). [full citation needed]

Later Crowley commented that obeah is the magical acts and wanga the words.

Ozzy Osbourne

Ozzy Osbourne (1948-) is an English musician. He was in the heavy metal band Black Sabbath until 1979. His nickname is The Prince of Darkness.

Osbourne's music has occult themes and he has been accused of corrupting teenagers with "satanic music". In the past he was compared to Aleister Crowley because of his occult imagery and occult lyrics in his music and performances.

On Osbourne's first solo album he had a song entitled Mr. Crowley. The song was rated the 23rd greatest heavy metal song of all time. Osbourne wrote the song after reading a book about Crowley. The song was written to play up to Osbourne's occult image. In the song Osbourne alludes to Crowley's drug use and controversy.

The last verse states:

"Was it polemically sent
I want to know what you meant".

P

Paintings

Crowley produced a number of artworks during his life. He painted landscapes, portraits and trance paintings.

It is said that his art was inspired by German expressionism, surrealism and symbolism. Artists who influenced Crowley's art include Wassily Kandinsky, Georges Rouault and Paul Gaugin. He took up painting as hobby in New York in 1919.

Jack Parsons

Jack Parsons (1914-1952) was a rocket scientist and follower of Crowley's beliefs. Parson's invented the first rocket engine which used a castable composite rocket propellant. He also worked on the creation of solid and liquid fuel rockets.

As a young boy he developed an interest in occultism, once scaring himself during a ritual to try and invoke the devil to appear in his bedroom. Parsons was involved in numerous far left activities as a rocket scientist.

In 1939 he attended the Church of Thelma in Hollywood to watch The Gnostic Mass. Parsons was interested in Crowley's writings, linking Thelmic magick to quantum physics.

Parsons gave most of his salary to the O.T.O. and experimented with drugs and sex. In the 1940s Parson's became friends with L. Ron Hubbard who would later found Scientology. Parsons was forced by the US government to sell his shares in his rocket company. He bought a house as a base for the O.T.O. and embarked on various magic experiments. He tried to incarnate a Goddess on Earth.

Crowley did not approve of these experiments saying "Suspect Ron Hubbard playing confidence trick—Jack Parsons weak fool—obvious victim prowling swindlers." Hubbard ran off with $20,000 of Parson's money and his girlfriend.

Parson's worked on making explosive props for movies. Parsons later blew up himself while preparing explosives for a movie prop job.

Poetry

Crowley wrote numerous poems during his life and published many collections of poetry. Some were obscene which got him into trouble with the authorities. Some gained critical success; other reviews were mixed. His poetry collections were never big sellers and many were published by Crowley himself.

Influences on his poetry were naturally occult mythology and the occult. William Blake was one big influence on his work.

Herbert Charles Pollitt

3Herbert Charles Pollitt (July 20, 1871 – 1942) was patron of the arts and a stage female impersonator. He had a relationship with Crowley.

Pollitt attended Trinity College, Cambridge

University between 1889-1896. In 1897 Pollitt
went back to Cambridge to perform his as a
female at the Cambridge Footlights. He met
Crowley and the two started a relationship.
Crowley later stated: "I lived with Pollitt as his
wife for some six months and he made a poet out
of me."

The two broke up as Pollitt was not interested in
the occult and mysticism. Later in Crowley's book
The Confessions of Aleister Crowley, published in
1929 Crowley called the break up "lifelong
regret".

Crowley discussed his relationship with Pollitt in
his 1910 book on homosexual love Scented
Garden of Abdullah the Satirist of Shiraz.

Q

Qabalah

Qabalah is a western mystic tradition of magical
teachings and knowledge. It is derived from
Kabbalah, an ancient Jewish mystical tradition.
Teachings are on topics such as the nature of
divinity, the role of humans of Earth, the fate of
the soul, astrology, tarot and other mystic
practices.

Crowley was involved in two forms of Qabalah.

English Qaballa

English Qaballa is a Qabalah system discovered by James Lees in 1976. Lees developed the system in an attempt to understand Crowley's book The Book of the Law. It is a system of arithmetic that interprets the letters in the English alphabet with an assigned set of values.

Jake Stratton said of the system:

"the English Qaballa is a qabalah and not a system of numerology. A qabalah is specifically related to three factors: one, a language; two, a 'holy' text or texts; three, mathematical laws at work in these two."

Crowley intended the book to have an English Qabalah developed from it. In verse 2:55 Crowley wrote:

"Thou shalt obtain the order & value of the English Alphabet, thou shalt find new symbols to attribute them unto"

Lees got the order and value by the diagonally hand written page verse Ch. III, v. 47 in Liber AL vel Legis, The Book of the Law.

Hermetic Qabalah

Hermetic Qabalah is a Western esoteric occult tradition, which developed from studies of Jewish

Kabalah. It provides the framework and underlying philosophy for Crowley related occult societies the Golden Dawn and Thelemic societies. It is a precursor to modem Pagan, New Age and Wicca movements.

Crowley used Hermetic magick frequently. For example Crowley's book Liber 777 (published in 777 and Other Qabalistic Writings of Aleister Crowley) was influenced by the Panthiesism of Hermetic Qabalah and the book relates magic to the ten Sehiroth speheres.

In The Templeo of Soloma Crowley wrote:

"Fortunately, there is one science that can aid us, a science that, properly understood by the initiated mind, is as absolute as mathematics, more self-supporting than philosophy, a science of the spirit itself, whose teacher is God, whose method is simple as the divine Light, and subtle as the divine Fire, whose results are limpid as the divine Water, all-embracing as the divine Air, and solid as the divine Earth. Truth is the source, and Economy the course, of that marvellous stream that pours its living waters into the Ocean of apodeictic certainty.

The Truth that is infinite in its infinity as the primal Truth which which it is identical is infinite in its Unity.

Need we say that we speak of the holy Qabalah?

O science secret, subtle, and sublime, who shall name thee without veneration, without prostration of soul, spirit, and body before thy divine Author, without exaltation of soul, spirit, and body as by His favour they bathe in His lustral and illimitable Light?"

Quotes

Here are some of Crowleys's famous quotes:

Sit still. Stop thinking. Shut up. Get out!

Eight Lectures on Yoga

Every man and every woman is a star.

I am divided for love's sake, for the chance of union

There is no law beyond Do what thou wilt

The Book of the Law

There is a single main definition of the object of all magical Ritual. It is the uniting of the Microcosm with the Macrocosm.

Magick in Theory and Practice (1929)

I believe in one Gnostic and Catholic Church of Light, Life, Love and Liberty, the Word of whose

Law is THELEMA

There is no part of me that is not of the gods!

Gnostic Mass

The people who have really made history are the martyrs.

As long as sexual relations are complicated by religious, social and financial considerations, so long will they cause all kinds of cowardly, dishonourable and disgusting behaviour.

To read a newspaper is to refrain from reading something worth while.

Modern morality and manners suppress all natural instincts, keep people ignorant of the facts of nature and make them fighting drunk on bogey tales....

The Confessions of Aleister Crowley

As soon as you put men together, they somehow sink, corporatively, below the level of the worst of the individuals composing it.

Magick Without Tears

know thy self and ones limits.

I may be a Black Magician but I'm a bloody great one.

R

Racism

Was Aleister Crowley a racist or a white supremacist? This has been debated by historians and scholars of Crowley. He lived in an era when racism was commonplace and normal, and even if a white person of the time was not racist they still may have felt that those non-white people in places such as colonies were inferior or not as advanced as white people. He used many words which are considered offensive today in his writings and fiction. But this was normal in many other writings of his era. One explanation is that Crowley was fond of making fun of people and insulting them. He used racial slurs as a part of this.

Crowley was friends with the black equality and anti-racist campaigner Nancy Cunard. Cunard stated that he was appalled at Hitler's treatment of the Jews. In many of his writings in his travels to places such as China, Mexico and North Africa he often praises the populations and states that he has an affinity with their culture.

As always with Crowley there are numerous layers to his views on race, mainly because he wrote a great deal of varied material in his life.

Theodor Reuss

Theodor Reuss (June 28, 1855 – October 28, 1923) was a German-British occultist. Other occupations were police agent, singer and journalist.

He was a Freemason and a head of the Ordo Templi Orientis (O.T.O). Reuss was born in Augsburg, Germany. In 1876 he became a Freemason in Pilger Loge No. 238 of the United Grand Lodge of England. Reuss was expelled from the English Socialist League in 1886 after being accused of being a German police spy. In 1895 Reuss had discussions with Carl Kellner to form the O.T.O. In 1902 the two agreed to work with leading Freemasons to establish the Order.

In 1910 Reuss lived in London and met Crowley. Reuss made Crowley VII° of O.T.O in 1910, then in 1912 he made Crowley IX° and gave him the title of National Grand Master General X° for the O.T.O. in the United Kingdom of Great Britain and Ireland. In 1913 Crowley wrote his Gnostic Mass for Reuss's Gnostic Catholic church. Crowley dedicated his book The Giant's Thumb (a 1915 collection of poetry) and The Ship (a play written in 1913) to Reuss.

Reuss was active in the occult world writing - such as translating Crowley's works into German - and setting up several organizations. At the World Federation of Universal Freemasonry in Zurich in

1920 he suggested that Thelema should become the official religion for all members.

He suffered a stroke in 1920. Crowley wrote to people suggesting that Reuss was ill and giving O.T.O. degrees to unsuitable people. Reuss found out and distanced the O.T.O. from Thelema in a letter to Crowley. In response Crowly proclaimed himself head of the O.T.O - Frater Superior, and Outer Head of the Order. later stated that Reuss confirmed Crowley as O.T.O. head, but no correspondence or evidence confirming this has been found.

Reuss died in 1923.

Rose Edith Kelly

Rose Edith Kelly (1874-1932) was an Englishwoman who was married to Crowley between 1903 and 1909.

Crowley married Kelly to save her from an arranged marriage. But after marrying they grew closer.

On their honeymoon in Egypt in 1904 he let Rose direct him in a magic ritual and this led him to hearing voices from Aiwass, which were written down and became the key Thelemeite text The Book of the Law.

Kelly and Crowley had two daughters: Lilith (1904-06) and Lola Zara (1907-90). The divorced in 1909. Rose married Dr Joseph Andrew Gormley in 1912.
She died in 1932.

Auguste Rodin

Auguste Rodin (12 November 1840 – 17 November 1917) was a French sculptor. He is known as the founder of modern sculpture responsible for such sculptures as The Thinker, The Kiss and The Gates of Hell.

Crowley became friends with Rodin in Paris in 1902 when he moved to Paris. In 1903 Crowley released a collection of poems inspired by Rodin artwork entitled Rodin in Rome.

The book includes lithographs given by Rodin to Crowley.

Royal Leamington Spa

Aleister Crowley was born in Royal Leamington Spa. Royal Leamington Spa is a town in Warwickshire, England. He was born at 30 Clarendon Square. In 1880 Crowley moved with his family to Redhill in Surrey.

S

Satan

Crowley has often been called a Satanist. He stated that he was not a Satanist, although on occasion he played up to sensationalist newspaper stories which described him as a dangerous Satanist. Crowley did not accept the Christian world view, and therefore for him Satan did not exist. Crowley wrote that the devil does not exist and is merely a label for a God that someone dislikes.

Crowley's occult image and works have been considered to have influenced modern Satanists. Crowley used Satanic icons and rhetoric. For example Crowley described himself as the Beast 666 and referred to the whore of Babylon. Crowley's lifestyle was in line with Satanic beliefs. But there is not much specific Satanic influence or content in Crowley's writings. Crowley was instead interested in numerous other of the occult and alternative religious beliefs.

School

Aged 8 Crowley was sent to H.T. Habershon's Christian boarding school. This was an evangelical school in Hastings. He then attended the Ebor preparatory school in Cambridge. It was run by Reverend Henry d'Arcy. Crowley later stated stated that he considered the Reverend d'Arcy to be a sadist. After short spells at Malvern College and Tonbridge School Crowley lived with a tutor from the Brethren Christian sect of his parents in Eastbourne. He also attended chemistry courses at Eastbourne College.

777 and Other Qabalistic Writings of Aleister Crowley

777 and Other Qabalistic Writings of Aleister Crowley is a book of papers published by Crowley. It was edited by Israel Regardie and published in 1973.

The book is a reference book made up of tables based on the Hermetic Qabalah, and a table of magical correspondences. It contains Gematria, which explains Qabalah taught by the Hermetic Order of the Golden Dawn. Liber 777 has 191 columns with each row corresponding to a Sephirah or path on the Tree of Life.

Sepher Sephiroth is a list of numbers from 1-3321 and their Hebrew word equivalents.

Sex Magic

Sex Magic is a form of sex used in religious,

magic, ritualistic and spiritual acts. Sexual energy is used to transcend reality. Crowley though restrictions on sexual expression meant the subconscious mind could not be freed. Crowley introduced sex magic in the highest degrees in the O.T.O.

There were three teachings of three degrees:

VIII°: masturbatory or autosexual magical techniques were taught, referred as the Lesser Work of Sol

IX°: heterosexual magical techniques were taught

XI°: anal intercourse magical techniques were taught.

Crowley called sex magic "the supreme magical power. Sex acts could be used during magic to achieve a goal such as creative success or making money.

During sex magic rituals a biscuit (a Cake of Light) containing semen, vaginal and menstrual fluids was used as a Eucharist.

St Petersburg

In 1997 Crowley travelled to St Petersburg in Russia. He intended to learn Russia as when at Cambridge University he intended to enter the diplomatic service.

Sgt. Pepper's Lonely Hearts Club Band

Sgt. Pepper's Lonely Hearts Club Band is an album by British music group The Beatles. It was released in 1967.

The cover of the album has a tableau of celebrities and historical people - 71 in all; Crowley is one of them. It was designed by pop artists Jann Haworth and Peter Blake.

Crowley can be seen on the cover between Indian guru Sri Yukteswar and the Hollywood star Mae West.

Wilfred Talbot Smith

Wilfred Talbot Smith (1995-1957) was a ceremonial magician and occultist from England. He was born in Tonbridge in England and moved to Canada in 1907. He became interested in western esotericism, yoga and eastern religion and this led him to join the A∴A∴ in 1912. He later joined the O.T.O. and in 1915 met Crowley after Crowley visited the O.T.O. lode in British Columbia in Canada.

In 1922 Smith moved to Los Angeles and continued his activities in the O.T. O and A∴A∴.. In

1932 Crowley fell ill in England. He sent Smith a testament stating that if Crowley died Smith would take over from Crowley as Frater Superior and Outer Head of the Order (OHO) of the O.T.O. Crowley recovered from his illness.

In 1934 Smith annoyed Crowley by incorporating the Church of Thelema in the US. Crowley thought Smith had incorporated the O.T.O., but the O.T.O. remained an unincorporated secret society. The confusion over the matter led Crowley and Smith to fall out for a period.

Smith founded the Agape Lodge No 1 in Hollywood which became a very active group for Thelema followers. There were numerous controversies in the Lodge with FBI investigations.

Smith fell out with leading members of the lodge and Crowley himself as Crowley supported other members during disagreements at the lodge. In 1942 Crowley studied Smith' s astrological birth chart and concluded that Smith was the incarnation of God. Soon Smith complained to Crowley about the behaviour of other members stating "Would to God you knew your people better." This led the two to fall out again, and Crowley started spreading malicious gossip about Smith. Crowley insisted that Smith be shunned by other Lodge members.

Crowley died in 1947. Smith continued his Thelemic activities until his death in 1957.

Spying

Crowley mentioned in his book Confessions and Elsewhere that he undertook intelligence work in New York the USA between 1914-19 – during World War 1.

He was publicly working as an "anti-British propagandist" but was in reality a double agent working for the British government. He was paid to write pro-German articles in American newspapers such as The Fatherland. The Fatherland was edited by a German spy called George Sylvester Viereck. Its articles supported German neutrality in World War 1. Crowley wrote them in a ridiculous over the top pro-German style, which was intended to make the Germans look arrogant and cause people in the US to become anti-German. Crowley's detractors said he supported the German bombing of the ship Lusitania as it would keep the US out of the war. But Crowley thought it would help bring the US into the war.

Crowley worked with pro-Irish independence groups as part of his spying activities in the US who supported Germany as they opposed Britain.

Charles Stansfeld Jones

Charles Stansfeld Jones (1886–1950) was a ceremonial magician and occultist. His magic name was Frater Achad.

An accountant by trade, he joined the A∴A∴ in 1909. Jones took the Magister Templi obligation and became a Babe of the Abyss. Crowley also thought Jones had discovered a Kabbalistic key to The Book of the Law. Crowley thus regarded Jones as his Magical Child, and thought he was the child prophesied in The book of the Law.

Jones became a master of the temple in the O.T.O. Jones and Crowley experimented with the Ouija board and considered making their own version. Jones moved to Canada to work as an accountant and opened O.T.O. operations there, eventually resigning from the O.T.O.

Jones suffered a nervous breakdown, converted to Catholicism and tried to convert Thelema members

Star Sign

Crowley's star sign was Libra. He was born on October 12 1875. Librans are extroverted with charm and intelligence. They are concerned with gaining balance in the World.

Stockholm

In December 1896 Aleister Crowley took a holiday

in Stockholm. It is here he is said to have had his first mystical experience.

In Stockholm Crowley stayed at the Grand Hotel. Here he had an experience that in his his own words

" `awakened [him] to the knowledge that I possessed a magical means of becoming conscious of and satisfying a part of my nature which had up to that moment concealed itself from me. It was an experience of horror and pain, combined with a certain ghostly terror, yet at the same time it was the key to the purest and holiest spiritual ecstasy that exists."

Crowley went ice skating and met a Scottish man - or a man he thought to be Scottish, by the name of James L. Dickson. On the stroke of New Year's Eve Crowley had sex with Dickson. It was his first such experience and resulted in a "mystical" experience.

The Stratagem and other Stories

The Stratagem and other Stories is a collection of short stories written by Crowley and published in 1929.

The stories are The Stratagem, The Testament of Magdalen Blair and His Secret Sin. Joseph Conrad gave the Stratagem a good review.

The inscription at the start of the book read:

"To the Memories of Three Dead Friends: Joseph Conrad, who applauded the first story; Allan Bennett, Bhikku Ananda Metteya, who suggested the second, and Eugene John Weiland, who bowled me out over the third."

T

Therion

Therion is a deity found in Thelema. Therion evolved from The Beast from the Book of Revelation. Crowley would often refer to himself as Master Therion.

Therion's female counterpart is Babalon.

Thoth Tarot

The Thoth Tarot is a tarot deck devised by Crowley. Instructions on how to use the deck was given in his 1944 book The Book of Thoth. It took Crowley five years - between 1938 and 1943 to complete the project.

The illustrations on the tarot cards include imagery from science, philosophy and other occult systems. Several of the trumps were renamed. The astrological, numerical and Hebrew alphabet correspondences of 4 trumps were re arranged.

The illustrations were painted by Lady Freida Harris, who also also had considerable input in the content and promotion of the tarot deck.

Tutankhamun

Tutankhamun (1341 - 1323 BC) was an ancient Egyptian Pharaoh who ruled from 1332-1323. He is also commonly known as King Tut.

In 1922 his tomb was excavated by British Egyptology Howard Carter. Many artifacts and the famous Tutankhamun mask were found In the tomb. Some excavating the tomb died in mysterious circumstances leading some to believe it was part of a Pharaoh's curse: 20 people died.

For example, Captain Richard Bethell was found dead in a Mayfair club: he had been suffocated wit a pillow. Lord Westbury fell to his death in his apartment from 7 floors up.

Some have suggested that Crowley was killing the Egyptologists in a series of ritualistic murders because they had performed a sacrilegious act.

U

Unicursal hexagram

The Unicursal hexagram is a six pointed star that is draw unicursally. In Thelema the hexagram has a five petalled flower in the middle. The hexagram symbolises a pentangle and is similar to the Rosicrucian Rose Cross or Egyptian Ankh.

It represents microcosmic forces: pentangle, pentrgram, pentagrammaton, Yahshuah and macro-cosmic forces: hexagram, heavenly cosmic forces and divine.

V

Karl von Eckartshausen

Karl von Eckartshausen (28 June 1752 – 12 May 1803) was a German mystic and philosopher. He wrote the Christian mystic book The Cloud upon the Sanctuary. This book was popular among Hermetic Order of the Golden Dawn members. It is said to have inspired Crowley to join the Golden Dawn.

Crowley was interested in the book's idea of an Interior church - the inward conception of spiritual things, or spiritual experience rather than doctrine.

Virginity

Crowley stated that he lost his virginity aged 14 with a maid.

The Vision and the Voice

The Vision and the Voice is a book by Crowley. It tells of Crowley's mystical journey as he explores the 30 Enochian aethyrs which Edward Kelley and John Dee developed in the 1500s.

The book was written from two visions Crowley had in Mexico in 1900 and Algeria in 1909.

W

Leila Waddell

Leila Waddell (1880-32) was an Australian violinist and occultists. She was associated with Crowley and was one of his Scarlet Women.

Waddell was performing in the theatre in London in 1908 and met Crowley. They studied the occult and mystical matters together. They also took mescaline. Crowley called Waddell Laylah and she is mentioned by this name in The Book of Lies (1912) and The Confessions of Aleister Crowley. The Book of Lies was devoted to her and a photograph of Waddell during a ritual is in the book. Other names Crowley had for Waddell were Divine Whore, Mother of Heaven and Whore of Babylon.

Waddell was a distinguished writer on the occult and magician. She took part in Crowley's Rites if Eleusis ritual performance at Caxton Hall in 1910. Crowley was was inspired to mix magic, music and dance by Waddell's violin performances.

She co-authored Magick (Book4) with Crowley mainly by asking questions of Crowley; his responses made up the content. In 1915 Crowley made a speech supporting Irish independence at the statue of Liberty. Waddell accompanied him on the violin. Crowey promoted a seven member female violin group containing Waddell called the Ragged Ragtime Girls. The group toured America, Russia and Europe.

In 1923 she returned to Sydney in Australia, joined the JC Williamson Ltd and Conservatorium and Philharmonic Societies Orchestras and resumed music teaching at the Convent School of the Sacred Heart in Sydney's Elizabeth Bay. She passed away in 1932.

A.E. Waite

A.E. Waite (2 October 1857 – 19 May 1942) was a British poet and occult writer. He was the first to create a systematic study of western occultism and co created the Rider-Waite tarot deck. In 1991 he joined the Hermetic Order of the Golden Dawn, leaving in 1914.

In March 1898, Crowley obtained A.E. Waite's The Book of Black Magic and of Pacts and because it mentioned a hidden church. Crowley later became hostile towards Waite because of the "arrogant" style and hidden grammar of Waite's writings."

Oscar Wilde

Oscar Wilde said of Crowley "Aleister Crowley has been a guest at every Great House in England ... once.".

Although Crowley and Wilde never met, they mixed in the same social circles and Crowley was an admirer of Wilde. Crowley was annoyed that a monument sculpted by Jacob Epstein at Wilde's Paris tome had the genitals covered up by a bronze butterfly. Crowley removed the butterfly.

White Stains

White Stains is a book of poetry written by

Crowley and published in 1898 in Amsterdam, The Netherlands. it consists of a collection of poems in French and English. Most are obscenely sexual in nature. The title of the book refers to masturbation.

100 copies were printed - most were destroyed by British Customs in 1924.

Louis Wilkinson

Louis Wilkinson (1881-66) was a British writer. He often wrote using the name Louis Marlow. In 1907 he met Crowley. They became friends in 1915 when they were both living in America. Wilkinson was not a student of Crowley's occult views, and even said that he vary rarely discussed magic with Crowley. He said he admired Crowley:

"My chief feeling about him is one of personal gratitude, for I have known very few who, as persons, have impressed me more or rewarded me more than he did".

In 1945 an increasingly frail Crowley needed a retirement home. Wilkinson found Crowley a place at Netherwood in Hastings, England. Crowley died in 1947. Wilkinson was one of the estate's three executors. At the funeral at Brighton crematorium Wilkinson read from the Hymn of Pan, Book of the Law and Gnostic Mass. Wilkinson discussed Crowley in Seven Friends - a book published in

1953 about Wilkinson's most interesting friends.

Jane Wolfe

Jane Wolfe (1875-58) was an American actress and associate of Crowley. She was a popular character actress, particularly in silent films between 1910-20.

She became interested in occult and magic and in 1919 started to correspond with Crowley. Aged 45 she gave up her film career to join Crowley at his magic commune Abbey of Thelema in Sicily. She wrote a detailed account of life and her activities there in The Cefalu Diaries. After the Abbey closed down in 1923 she worked for Crowley in London and Paris. In 1935 she helped found the Agape Lodge O.T.O. lodge in Los Angeles, becoming its Lodge master.

World War 2

During World War 2 Crowley was in London - with spells living in in Torquay and Buckinghamshire.

Naturally Crowley was fascinated by Nazism. It is said that he though Hitler was a potential recruit for his Thelema religion.

But Nazi Germany abolished the O.T.O., and Crowley attacked Hitler calling him a black magician. Crowley offered his services to the British Naval Intelligence division, but they said they had no need for him.

During the war Crowley did associate with famous figures such as Dennis Wheatley, Roald Dahl and Ian Fleming. Crowley later claimed to have invented the V for victory sign. Crowley published a book about Tarot cards called The Book of Thoth in 1944. A book on the rights of humanity Liber Oz and a poem about the liberation of France called Le Gauloise were also published.

X

XXX - Liber Librae, The Book of Balance

Liber Librae, The Book of Balance is a Karmic Yoga book by Crowley intended to be a course of morality suitable for the average man.

Y

W. B. Yeats

W. B. Yeats (13 June 1865 – 28 January 1939) was an Irish poet and writer. Yeats was from a Protestant background but an advocate of Irish

nationalism. He had a keen interest in the occult
and mysticism which influenced some of his
poetry. His interest in the occult resulted in him
becoming acquainted with Crowley.

In 1890 he joined the Hermetic Order of the
Golden Dawn. In 1892 he wrote "The mystical life
is the centre of all that I do and all that I think
and all that I write". When Crowley and Yeats
were members of the Golden Dawn they had a
few feud due to Crowley's insistence on using
magic for evil purposes. Yeats used white magic -
good magic - against Crowley when Crowley
wanted to conduct black magic rituals at the
Dawn headquarters. In one incident in 1900 Yeats
and other white magicians ejected Crowley from
the Golden Dawn building which was later called
the Battle of Blythe Road.

Crowley Bibliography

777 and Other Qabalistic Writings of Aleister Crowley: Including Gematria & Sepher Sephiroth. (1982).
Aha!: Being Liber CCXLII. (1996).
Aleister Crowley and the Practice of the Magical Diary. (2006).
Amrita : Essays in Magical Rejuvenation. (1990)
"The Blue Equinox" (Equinox III:1). (1992)
The Book of the Law (1997).
The Book of Lies, which is also falsely called Breaks, originally (1912).
The Book of Thoth: A Short Essay on the Tarot of the Egyptians (1944)
Clouds without Water. (1909)
Collected Works of Aleister Crowley 1905-1907. (1974)
Commentaries on the Holy Books and Other Papers (Equinox IV:1). (1996)
The Confessions of Aleister Crowley: An Autohagiography. (1979)
Crowley on Christ. (1974)
Diary of a Drug Fiend. (1970)
Eight Lectures on Yoga (Equinox III:4). (1985)
Enochian World of Aleister Crowley: Enochian Sex Magick. (1991)
The Equinox (I:1-10). (2006)
The Equinox (III:10). (2001)
The Equinox of the Gods (Equinox III:3). (1992)
Gems from the Equinox. (1982)
The General Principles of Astrology (Liber DXXXVI). (2002)

The Goetia: The Lesser Key of Solomon the King.
(1995)
The Heart of the Master. (1973)
The Holy Books of Thelema (Equinox III:9).
(1983)
Khing Kang King: The Classic of Purity, Being
Liber XXI. (1980)
Konx Om Pax: Essays in Light. (1990)
The Law is for All: The Authorized Popular
Commentary of Liber AL vel Legis sub figura
CCXX, The Book of the Law. (1996)
Liber Aleph vel CXI: The Book of Wisdom or Folly
(Equinox III:6). (1991)
Little Essays Toward Truth. (1991)
The Magical Diaries of Aleister Crowley: Tunisia
1923. (1996)
The Magical Record of the Beast 666: The Diaries
of Aleister Crowley, 1914-1920. (1972)
Magick: Liber ABA, Book Four, Parts I-IV. (1997)
Magick Without Tears. [First Edition 1973] (1982)
Moonchild. (1972)
The Qabalah of Aleister Crowley: Three Texts.
(1973)
The Revival of Magick and Other Essays. (1998)
Rites of Eleusis: As Performed at Caxton Hall.
(1990)
The Scrutinies of Simon Iff. (1987)
Shih Yi: A critical and mnemonic paraphrase of
the Yi King by Ko Yuen (Equinox III:8). (1971).
The Spirit of Solitude. (1929)(The first two
volumes of an intended six of Crowley's
autobiography. The six volumes appeared in
omnibus form as The Confessions of Aleister
Crowley: An Autohagiography in 1989)

The Stratagem and other Stories. (1929)
Tannhäuser : A Story of All Time. (1974)
The Tao Teh King: A New Translation (Equinox
III:8). (1976)
The Vision & the Voice: With Commentary and
Other Papers (Equinox IV:II). (1998)
The World's Tragedy. (1985)

Poetry

Aceldama, A Place to Bury Strangers In. (1974)
Ahab, and Other Poems. (1974)
Aleister Crowley: Selected Poems. (1986)
The Argonauts. (1974)
Clouds without Water. (1974)
Gargoyles: Being Strangely Wrought Images of
Life and Death. (1974)
Golden Twigs. (1988)
Jephthah. (1974)
Jezebel, and Other Tragic Poems. (1974)
Orpheus: A Lyrical Legend. (1974)
The Scented Garden of Abdullah the Satirist of
Shiraz(1991)
Snowdrops from a Curate's Garden. (1986)
Songs for Italy.
Songs of the Spirit. (1974)
The Soul of Osiris: Comprising the Temple of The
Holy Ghost and The Mother's Tragedy. (1974)
The Star and the Garter. (1974)
The Sword of Song: Called by Christians, The
Book of the Beast. (1974)
White Stains. (1973)
The Winged Beetle. (1992)

www.ingramcontent.com/pod-product-compliance
Lightning Source LLC
Chambersburg PA
CBHW031431130726
47989CB00003B/1083